THE
VISION
STATEMENT

9 INTERACTIVE BIBLE STUDIES FOR
SMALL GROUPS AND INDIVIDUALS

GREG CLARKE

matthiasmedia

The Vision Statement
Second edition
© Matthias Media 2010

First published 2003

Matthias Media
(St Matthias Press Ltd ACN 067 558 365)
PO Box 225
Kingsford NSW 2032
Australia
Telephone: (02) 9663 1478; international: +61-2-9663-1478
Facsimile: (02) 9663 3265; international: +61-2-9663-3265
Email: info@matthiasmedia.com.au
Internet: www.matthiasmedia.com.au

Matthias Media (USA)
Telephone: 724 964 8152; international: +1-724-964-8152
Facsimile: 724 964 8166; international: +1-724-964-8166
Email: sales@matthiasmedia.com
Internet: www.matthiasmedia.com

ISBN 978 1 921441 62 2

Cover design and typesetting by Matthias Media.
Series concept design by Lankshear Design Pty Ltd.

» CONTENTS

ACKNOWLEDGEMENTS
These studies have been developed by Greg Clarke, some
of them from sermons given by Philip Jensen in Kuantan,
Malaysia in 1997. Our thanks to Adam Road Presbyterian
Centre and Prinsep Street Presbyterian Church for
supplying additional study material that accompanied
Philip's sermons and has been incorporated in some of
these studies.

REVELATION

»HOW TO MAKE THE MOST OF THESE STUDIES

1. What is an Interactive Bible Study?

Interactive Bible Studies are a bit like a guided tour of a famous city. They take you through a particular part of the Bible, helping you to know where to start, pointing out things along the way, suggesting avenues for further exploration, and making sure that you know how to get home. Like any good tour, the real purpose is to allow you to go exploring for yourself—to dive in, have a good look around, and discover for yourself the riches that God's word has in store.

In other words, these studies aim to provide stimulation and input and point you in the right direction, while leaving you to do plenty of the exploration and discovery yourself.

We hope that these studies will stimulate lots of 'interaction'—interaction with the Bible, with the things we've written, with your own current thoughts and attitudes, with other people as you discuss them, and with God as you talk to him about it all.

2. The format

Each study contains five main components:

- sections of text that introduce, inform, summarize and challenge
- a set of numbered study questions that help you examine the passage and think through its meaning
- sidebars that provide extra bits of background or optional extra study ideas, especially regarding other relevant parts of the Bible
- 'Implications' sections that help you think about what these passages mean for you and your life today
- suggestions for thanksgiving and prayer as you close.

3. How to use these studies on your own

- Before you begin, pray that God would open your eyes to what he is saying in the Bible, and give you the spiritual strength to do something about it.
- Work through the study, reading the text, answering the questions about the Bible passage, and exploring the sidebars as you have time.
- Resist the temptation to skip over the 'Implications' and 'Give thanks and pray' sections at the end. It is important that we not only hear and understand God's word, but respond to it. These closing sections help us do that.
- Take what opportunities you can to talk to others about what you've learnt.

4. How to use these studies in a small group

- Much of the above applies to group study as well. The studies are suitable for structured Bible study or cell groups, as well as for more informal pairs and triplets. Get together with a friend or friends and work through them at your own pace; use them as the basis for regular Bible study with your spouse. You don't need the formal structure of a 'group' to gain maximum benefit.

- For small groups, it is *very useful* if group members can work through the study themselves *before* the group meets. The group discussion can take place comfortably in an hour (depending on how sidetracked you get!) if all the members have done some work in advance.
- The role of the group leader is to direct the course of the discussion and to try to draw the threads together at the end. If you are a group leader, the material in the appendix 'Tips for leaders' will help you think through how to use these studies in a group setting.
- If your group members usually don't work through the study in advance, it's extra important that the leader prepares which parts to concentrate on, and which parts to glide past more quickly. In particular, the leader will need to select which of the 'Implications' to focus on.
- We haven't included an 'answer guide' to the questions in the studies. This is a deliberate move. We want to give you a guided tour of the Bible, not a lecture. There is more than enough in the text we have written and the questions we have asked to point you in what we think is the right direction. The rest is up to you.

5. Bible translation

Previous studies in our Interactive Bible Study series have assumed that most readers would be using the New International Version of the Bible. However, since the release of the English Standard Version in 2001, many have switched to the ESV for study purposes. For this reason, we have decided to quote from and refer to the ESV text, which we recommend.

» STUDY 1

BEHOLD THE KING

[REVELATION 1]

1. What excites you about studying the book of Revelation? What worries you?

IT IS TEMPTING TO SAY AT THE outset of these studies on Revelation that it is a difficult book to understand—one that has baffled and divided Christians down through the ages.

But this isn't strictly true. It is true that Revelation seems unfamiliar to 21st-century readers. It contains highly symbolic language, strange fantasy-like imagery and cosmic spiritual events. It seems disconnected from history in a way that the rest of New Testament is not. However, if you know the gospel of Jesus Christ, and if you have read at least some of the Old Testament, Revelation need not seem so strange at all.

In fact, the book of Revelation contains more references to the Old Testament than any other New Testament book. It presents for us—often in dramatic, pictorial style—the same truths that the Gospels teach about Jesus and his relation to the world.

As we work through the book in these nine studies, we will be relying on the Bible itself to interpret Revelation's message. Many discussions of Revelation get caught up in particular details of history: in dates and Roman emperors and who the Antichrist might be. But these are often distractions from the actual teaching of the book,

STUDY 1 BEHOLD THE KING » **9**

which places Jesus Christ firmly at the centre. It is fascinating, and occasionally instructive, to look at these background details, but the power of God's word is not found there. It is found in the extraordinary revelation that "The kingdom of the world has become the kingdom of our Lord and of his Christ, and he shall reign forever and ever" (Rev 11:15). Above all, Revelation is a call to worship the King of kings.

Optional question

Verse 7 looks like a quote from the Old Testament. Can you track it down, or can you track down any Old Testament passages which are similar?

Read Revelation 1:1–8.

2. What do we learn from this passage about why Revelation was written?

3. What promise is made to us in verse 3?

4. List everything we learn about Jesus from these verses.

5. What has Jesus done for "his servants" (vv. 5-6)?

What kind of book is this?

WHEN YOU START TO READ A BOOK, it helps to have some idea of what kind of book it is. Is it a novel, an economics textbook, a street directory, or a diary? It is usually quite easy to see which category (or genre) a book fits into, and this helps us to understand what is written. It stops us making foolish errors, such as thinking that characters in a novel are actually historical figures or that we will get some relaxing holiday escapism from reading the street directory.

What kind of book is Revelation?

It might be a hard question to answer, were it not for the fact that John has given us plenty of cues as to its genre. It is first a *revelation*—that is, an 'unveiling' of something that was hidden. Revelation reveals a mystery to us—the mystery of what is happening in the heavenly realms. It gives us a window into heaven and the reality of God. Note, too, that it is 'the revelation', not 'revelations', as it is often mistakenly called.

The Greek word we translate as 'revelation' is **'apocalypse'**. 'Apocalypse' has come to have a wider meaning in contemporary culture, suggesting a great catastrophe or the end of the world, but in the Bible it simply means to reveal something that was hidden. This revelation has come 'down the line' from God to Jesus, from Jesus to his angel, from the angel to John, and from John to his readers (1:1-3).

Second, this book is a *prophecy*. John says so at the beginning (1:3) and end (22:7, 10, 18) of the book. The book records for us John's visions while on the island of Patmos, sent as a letter to "the seven churches", since he was not present himself to deliver God's word. As with all of God's prophets, John is revealing both the things "that are" (1:19) and "those that are to take place after this" (1:1, 19).

The third cue as to the nature of this book is found in Revelation 1:4. It is a *letter*, written "to the seven churches that are in Asia". From 1:4 to the end of the book is one long letter to these churches, sent as a

What is apocalyptic literature?

'Revelation' or 'apocalypse' refers to a kind of writing that was prominent during the period 300 BC to 200 AD (the book of Revelation was probably written towards the end of the first century AD). An apocalypse usually tells the story of a person's vision of another world, often a world of the future, where the secrets of reality are revealed and salvation is secured. It frequently contains images of the end of the world, heaven and hell, celestial beings and battles between them.

In the Old Testament, Daniel 7-12 and Zechariah 9-14 are apocalypses. ▶

Some examples of apocalypses outside the Bible include parts of 1 Enoch, 4 Ezra, and The Shepherd of Hermas. Our understanding of apocalyptic literature has been much improved by studying the Dead Sea Scrolls, which contain many apocalypses.

The style of this literature causes some difficulties for today's readers. But this need not be the case—it just requires us to remember what sort of writing we are dealing with. Apocalyptic writing is often dense with symbolism and highly stylized; it often refers to mythological figures and heroes from past ages; it will often be concerned with violence, vengeance, oppression and injustice. Its impact on us may be less logical than impressionistic, like a movie or abstract painting rather than an essay.

When we know this, it becomes easier to appreciate the overall message of apocalyptic writing without getting bogged down in the sometimes frustrating details.[1]

blessing to those who are waiting for the return of Christ. This helps us to place the letter in its historical context, and to be careful about the way in which we apply it to our own situation. It is certainly written for us, as is all Scripture, but we are not its original readers and we have to remain mindful of this.

Perhaps the best summary description of the nature of this book is "a letter of prophecy written in apocalyptic style".

Read Revelation 1:9–20.

6. What was John told to do by the trumpet-like voice?

7. John's vision in verses 12-16 draws into play several Old Testament passages. Quickly read these passages to get a feel for the connections:

- Ezekiel 8:1-2

- Daniel 7:13-14

- Daniel 8:15-17

- Daniel 10:4-6

- Zechariah 4:1-4

8. What can we make of the fact that the man appears "in the midst of the lampstands"?

9. The symbolism of the stars and lampstands is explained by the man (one of the few places in Revelation where this is the case). From this explanation (v. 20), what can we conclude about the meaning of the vision?

The godlike man

As we have seen, in many places in the Old Testament, a godlike man appears who reveals 'reality' to the prophet. The man in Revelation 1:13ff fits this picture, and he reveals to John that he is the key-holder to life itself. It seems only appropriate that John fell down as if dead.

However, there is a great sense of comfort and security in this vision, and in this whole initial section of John's letter to the churches. The one who holds the key to life, who has himself conquered death (1:18), is standing with the churches and holds their angels in his hand. How wonderful to have such a one on your side! As John said earlier, Jesus (for who else could the figure possibly represent?) *loves* his people, and has made them into a kingdom of servants who receive "grace" and "peace" (1:4) because they are loved by their Lord. Although the vision frightens John, it is also his great comfort, as he suffers on the island of Patmos, to know that the living one does not wish him to be afraid. It is as CS Lewis described the Christlike Aslan in his Narnia books: "Who said anything about safe? 'Course he isn't safe. But he's good. He's the King, I tell you."[2]

A book to read aloud

Revelation 1:3 tells us that this letter was intended to be read out loud. This can be a very valuable exercise for a small group to do, too, as it helps you to see (rather, to hear) how the book holds together and where the emphases lie.

You might like to try this before beginning the next study.

If you are in a small group, get one or two people to read the book aloud (it is a good idea to choose competent readers and not too many of them) while the others listen. Note down the way the structure of the book comes across, the significant themes, the striking images, and anything else that springs to mind.

To read the whole book in one sitting takes around one hour.

» Implications

(Choose one or more of the following to think about further or to discuss in your group.)

• It has already become clear that Revelation does not quote the Old Testament word for word, but tends to pull together different Old Testament images and concepts. Why do you think this might be the case? What does it tell us about the centrality of Jesus to the whole of Scripture?

• Is Revelation about the past, the present or the future? Discuss.

- How would you respond if someone said to you, "Revelation doesn't belong in the Bible because it doesn't teach the gospel"?

» Give thanks and pray

- Thank God for sending his angel to John so that this "testimony of Jesus Christ" was recorded for us to read today.
- Thank God for freeing us from our sins by the blood of Jesus.
- Ask God for wisdom over the coming weeks as you study the book of Revelation.

Endnotes

1. Further information can be found in good Bible dictionaries. For a sample of apocalyptic literature, see Mitchell Reddish (ed.), *Apocalyptic Literature: A reader*, Hendrickson, Peabody, Mass., 1995.
2. CS Lewis, *The Lion, the Witch and the Wardrobe*, The Chronicles of Narnia, HarperCollins, New York, 2005, p. 81.

THE SON OF MAN'S LETTER

[REVELATION 2:1–3:22]

1. Do you expect God to speak to you today? If so, what do you expect him to be concerned about?

ONE OF THE GREAT TRUTHS OF the Christian faith is, in the words of Francis Schaeffer, that "he is there and he is not silent". God not only exists, but also communicates with us in words that we can understand. He makes his requirements clear; he does not leave us in the dark. God is not dumb. The vision of the Son of Man that was given to John in Revelation 1 is another instance of God's generous communication—and this is a vision that speaks. The Son of Man also commands John to write down what he has seen and what he is told, in order that others can also hear the voice from heaven.

The Son of Man dictates a letter, which John is to publish abroad to those to whom it is addressed. Notice that although there are seven letters, they are each part of one larger letter which John is distributing to the churches (remember 1:4, 11). So the message that is given to each church is also read by the other churches. The letters are both real letters to real churches, addressing their particular concerns, and general letters to Christians everywhere. This is clear from the comment that recurs near the end of each letter: "He who has an ear, let him hear what the Spirit says to the *churches*" (e.g. 2:7).

Read Revelation 2:1–3:22.

2. In the table below, fill in the details of what is said to the churches. (If you are working in a group you may want to divide into smaller groups and allocate two churches to each group.)

To the angel of the church in ...	The words of ...	I know ...
Ephesus		
Smyrna		
Pergamum		
Thyatira		
Sardis		
Philadelphia		
Laodicea		

But ...	Challenge or warning ...	The one who conquers ...

3. Most promises to the church that overcomes or "conquers" refer to an event in a later part of Revelation (chapters 19-22). For example, compare the following verses:

- 2:7 with 22:2
- 2:26-27 with 19:15
- 3:12 with 22:4

What does this tell us about the future of those who "conquer"?

4. What do the following verses teach us about the nature of God as three persons? Revelation 2:7, 8, 27; 3:1, 5, 12b, 21.

One message

WE HAVE SEEN A STRONG PATTERN emerge in the seven letters given to the angels of the churches. There are differences between them, and the Son of Man addresses each of their specific situations. He leaves them in no doubt as to what is required of them. But what he says to each church is useful for every church. We might summarize the commands he makes as follows:

- If you have zeal without love: recover your love.
- If you are faithful but fearful: endure suffering for the crown of life which awaits you.
- If you are seduced by false teaching and immorality: repent.
- If you are lazy, asleep or dead in your faith: wake up, come back to life.
- If you are feeling weak and weary in your faith: remember that you will be rewarded and protected.
- If your obedience is lukewarm and you are complacent in faith: turn back and find your 'wealth' in Jesus.

One overall message emerges as a result of the pattern of the vision. That one message is this: remember who is in control. Do not be deceived into thinking that the world is all there is, that Jesus will not return as judge and king, that God does not have power. Do not let the troubles that come upon you in this evil age deceive you into thinking that God is not in control. He is. We know he is in control, because we know the one who has overcome evil. As Jesus told his disciples, "In the world you will have tribulation [or trouble]. But take heart; I have overcome the world" (John 16:33).

Although there are judgements and condemnations in these letters, they ought to be a source of encouragement to those who trust in the risen Christ. It is up to us to listen—to have 'ears to hear'—and then to obey.

» Implications

(Choose one or more of the following to think about further or to discuss in your group.)

- Someone says to you, "I wish I knew what Jesus wanted me to do. I wish he would give me a revelation!" How can you help them from Revelation 1-3?

- Which of the words of encouragement and warning given to the seven churches apply to your own church? What aspects of life threaten your church's ability to "conquer" the world?

- Should Christian churches today expect to suffer? Or should they expect to be triumphant and prosperous?

- A lot of scholarly effort has gone into understanding what these seven cities were like at the time the letter was written.[1] How important do you think such historical knowledge is to our understanding of this part of God's word?

- In the first column in the table on page 18, we saw a collection of descriptions about Jesus. How would you summarize what we are told about who Jesus is? How does this affect your attitude towards him?

» Give thanks and pray

- Thank God for being a holy and true God, and for being a God who does not judge without warning.
- Pray for your own church in light of your answers to the second implication question on the previous page.
- Pray for churches and Christians you know who are suffering; ask God to help them patiently endure.

Endnote
1. For instance, you can take a tour of the seven cities online:
   www.luthersem.edu/ckoester/Revelation/main.htm

THE OTHER REALITY

[REVELATION 4-5]

1. What images and ideas spring to mind when you think of heaven?

If you were going to choose just two chapters of the Bible from which to explain reality, Revelation 4 and 5 would do nicely. That may sound crazy—who understands the meaning of the crystal sea, the creatures around the throne, and the Lion of Judah? But this imagery all works together to communicate a very powerful and complete picture of who God is, what he has done and why it matters.

Having heard the message of the Son of Man to the seven churches, John looks once more at what is being revealed to him "in the Spirit on the Lord's day" (Rev 1:10). This time he is stunned to see an open door into heaven itself. The same voice—the voice of the Son of Man—introduces him to another vision.

Optional question

Quickly skim the following passages and note anything about the imagery that seems relevant to Revelation 4:

- Isaiah 6:1-7

Read Revelation 4:1-7.

2. In verse 1, the Son of Man shows John a vision of "what must take place after this". What is the "this" to which he is referring? (See 3:21.)

- Ezekiel 1

3. What impression are we given of the one who sits on the throne?

- Daniel 7:1-10

4. What kind of position do the 24 elders hold?

Read Revelation 4:8-11.

5. What are **the elders and the living creatures** doing?

6. Describe the ways this chapter depicts 'rulership'.

7. Why is the one on the throne worthy of worship?

The elders and living creatures

What are we to make of these unusual images? They are familiar from the Old Testament (Isaiah 6, Ezekiel 1, etc.), but they are also unique to this passage. They seem to be rich in symbolism, but we struggle to sort out how and what and why.

The elders are clearly rulers, in their white robes and gold crowns. Their number, 24, is suggestive: does it refer to the 12 tribes of Israel and the 12 "apostles of the Lamb" (as Revelation 21 calls them)? Or are they heavenly beings who somehow represent the church of God? We are not told.

Likewise, the four living creatures invoke Old Testament imagery. They have eyes everywhere; they seem to represent the creatures of the earth; they each have six wings— but we are not given more insight into the significance of these characteristics.

WHAT IS HEAVEN LIKE? IT IS ONE of the great questions of life. In this glorious chapter of the Bible, and throughout Revelation, we are given an insight into heaven, a vision of the way it is. It is worthwhile pausing and taking stock of how incredible this is.

Heaven is not just a time and place in the future; it is what is real *now*. If you understand what is now, you will have insight into what is then. John was given a vision of what must take place after the Son of Man has sat down at the throne with his Father (Rev 4:1). From the New Testament, we know that this has already taken place (Acts 2:33; Eph 1:20; Col 3:1; Heb 12:2; 1 Pet 3:22). Therefore, John's vision of the throne room of heaven is a vision of present reality. Heaven is the 'other reality', the one that we cannot yet see.

There is great reassurance in the Son of Man's words, that these things *must take place*. There are no doubts about the future—it is already set down. We are simply waiting for it to be revealed to all.

Behold the Lamb

Chapter 4 has presented a picture of what is happening in heaven. Chapter 5 presents a development in the scene. A new character is introduced: the slain Lamb, also known as the Lion of the tribe of Judah and the Root of David. At first, the appearance is shocking: what is a bloodied Lamb doing in heaven? But if we already know the good news of Jesus Christ, the one who died for our sins, we sense that this new dramatic development is crucial. And there is indication that the Lamb is powerful, too: it has many horns for strength, and many eyes for spiritual insight. It is unlike any other Lamb we have encountered.

Optional question

Read Isaiah 11:1-10 and note the similarities with Revelation 5.

Read Revelation 5.

8. What is John's role in the unfolding drama?

9. Why can't the scroll be opened (vv. 2-4)?

10. What is the reaction of the elders and living creatures when the Lamb takes the scroll from the right hand of the one on the throne (v. 8)?

11. What makes the Lamb worthy to open the scroll (vv. 9-10)?

12. What has the blood of the Lamb achieved? List at least three achievements.

THE SCENE IN THE THRONE ROOM of heaven, which looked so final in chapter 4, now takes a startling turn in chapter 5. Having seen the elders and living creatures fall before the throne and worship the Lord God Almighty, they now do the same thing *before the Lamb*. We need to pause and consider this extraordinary event. We know that God is the only one worthy of worship, for, as Revelation 4:11 told us, he created everything and everything owes its existence to him. Now, another figure is considered worthy of this devotion. The slain Lamb is to receive everything that belongs to the Lord God: power, wealth, wisdom, might, honour, glory and blessing. Revelation 5:13 confirms that the one on the throne and the Lamb will *share* in "blessing and honour and glory and might forever and ever!"

The drama has also stretched from heaven down to earth. The elders and the living creatures, who surround the throne in heaven, are joined by "every creature in heaven and on earth and under the earth" (5:13) in worshipping the Lamb. This is a brilliant pictorial summary of the relationship between God and his world. The Lamb was slain in order to ransom a people for God, and because of this the conquering Lamb shares in the glory of the Lord on the throne in heaven, and all creatures on heaven and earth sing their praises.

But we only know at this stage that the Lamb is worthy of praise, and worthy to open the seals on the scroll. We don't yet know what is written on that scroll. That is the subject of our next study.

» Implications

(Choose one or more of the following to think about further or to discuss in your group.)

- Are you ever tempted to think that God is not worthy of worship? What makes you think like this? How does Revelation 4 help us to understand God afresh?

- Do you live as if God is in fact ruling over all from his heavenly throne? What aspects of your life are challenged by this realization?

- Whereabouts in this picture are the original readers of John's letter? (Look back at Revelation 1:6.) Whereabouts in the picture do you place yourself?

- The 'hero' of Christian history is a slain Lamb. What might this teach us about the difference between human ideas of power and God's idea of power?

- Explore some of the Old Testament imagery relevant to this passage:
  - bowls of incense as prayers (Rev 5:8; cf. Ps 141:2)

  - the jewels of the throne room (Rev 4:3-4; cf. Ezek 1:26-28)

  - the seven eyes of God (Rev 5:6; cf. Zechariah 4)

- "The Bible doesn't tell us much about the future." From Revelation 4-5, how would you respond to such a comment?

- Could you summarize the gospel from Revelation 4 and 5? Try to write a one-paragraph summary, or explain it to a friend in a couple of minutes.

» Give thanks and pray

- Thank God for all that he has created (including us!).
- Praise and thank God for all that the slain Lamb has done.
- Ask for God's help in shaping your life according to the reality we see in Revelation 4-5.

OPENING THE SCROLL

[REVELATION 6:1–11:19]^{1}

1. What is your current view of the future of the world: optimistic, pessimistic or indifferent?

The history of the world

NOW AND THEN, SOMEONE TRIES to write a history of the world. *A Short History of the World* by Geoffrey Blainey devotes a long section to the importance of the discovery of fire. Its wide range of uses—for warmth, for driving away snakes, for sending smoke signals, for cremating the dead— reshaped the lives of all who used it. Such 'thematizing' of the experiences of hundreds of thousands of people gives us a way of looking at the past and making sense of a wide range of events and individuals.

It might seem ludicrous to try to summarize all the events, people and places that amass together to form the history of the world. And yet, it is in fact possible to do so. There are themes and stories which, when told carefully and skilfully, help us to understand who we are and where we have come from. They interpret our existence for us.

Revelation 6-11 is one such history of the world—one which comes to us from the very throne-room of heaven. It

Symbolism

The visions that Jesus gives to John are given in a dazzling array of symbols— strange beasts, significant numbers, falling stars, cosmic catastrophes with deeper meanings. Some people find the symbolism of Revelation exciting and meaningful; others baulk at it. However, we all use and recognize symbols every day. For example, everyone knows the meaning of those weird looking poles with the red, amber and green lights on them. Once you have used symbols for a while, they stop being strange and become second nature to you—a good reason for reading this book of the Bible regularly!

Some generalizations can be made about the symbols and imagery in Revelation:

1. Some of the symbols are explained. We should look to the Bible's own explanation of their meaning (e.g. Rev 1:20).

2. Not all images are symbols. A river can just be a river; it doesn't *have* to be a symbol of 'life' or 'change' or something else.

3. The symbols help us to understand the narrative (that is, the story). They provide pictures of what is happening. Our first task is not to find a meaning for the symbol ('What ▶

is revealed to John by none other than Jesus himself (remember Revelation 4:1). It has the imaginative richness of a dream, but it also unfolds quite recognizably as a story about what is happening in the world now, and what is going to take place.

As the Lamb opens the seals on the scroll that was given to him by God on the throne of heaven (see 5:7), scenes appear before John's eyes. They are scenes of horrific judgement—the unleashing of God's wrath on the earth and its sinful inhabitants. The scenes are conveyed to John in a series of **symbols**, in sets of seven. These symbols are not there to confuse us—on the contrary! They are provided to give us a 'feel' for God's unfolding judgement, to help us understand how it is to take place, and to give us a sense of how awesome, holy and complete it is.

Let's look at this unfolding story of judgement, and try to understand what God is revealing, and in what order it is taking place.

Read Revelation 6:1–8:5.

Read it quickly—don't dwell on the details (we'll come back to some of them). As you read, imagine the scenes that are described passing before your eyes in quick succession, a little like a music video clip.

2. What are the four riders on different coloured horses doing?

- White:

- Red:

- Black:

- Pale:

How would you summarize their activity?

3. What do the slain souls under the altar ask for (6:10)?

4. What answer is given to them in 6:11? (See Revelation 16:5-7 for later developments.)

other thing does this symbol represent?'), but to see how the symbol is working in the story ('How does this symbol play a part in the story?').

4. Some of the symbols may have been commonplace in the first century and only seem strange to us now.

5. There is consistent use of particular symbols throughout Scripture. Some of the most common, and widely agreed upon in terms of their meaning, are:

- 7: 'complete' or 'spiritually good'
- 4: 'everything' e.g. "the four corners of the earth" means 'the whole earth'
- 3½: 'incomplete' or 'prevented from completion'
- 6: 'spiritually bad'
- 12: 'a whole, united group' e.g. the twelve apostles
- white: 'victory, vindication, justice, righteousness'.

However, we can't assume that a symbol will mean the same thing in every situation. We still have to pay attention to the context of the sentence, paragraph and passage (see point 3).

6. When trying to understand a symbol's meaning in Revelation, think first of possible Old Testament allusions being made. ▶

Revelation is saturated with them. After that, it may be worthwhile turning to history, mythology and other literature for other possible allusions.

7. Symbols both conceal meaning and reveal it. The fact that they require thought and discussion doesn't mean that they are too hard to understand. They are just another means by which God can speak his word to us—one which requires some thinking, some imagining and some thinking again.

The sixth seal

Read Isaiah 2:12-22 and 34:4-8. What do these Old Testament references add to our understanding of the events of the sixth seal?

5. Summarize what happens when **the sixth seal** is opened (6:12-17). What does verse 17 call these events?

6. How does chapter 7 answer the question posed at the end of chapter 6?

7. The opening of the seventh seal leads to prayer offerings to God from "all the saints". From the angel's actions, what seems to be God's answer to the prayers (8:5)?

THE FOUR RIDERS ON DIFFERENT horses are doing their work here and now. We live in a world where might is right, where people kill each other, where many are starving and death reigns. This is how life is right now. We also empathize with the cries of the souls beneath the altar: how long, Lord, before you bring judgement on this wrongdoing? At the same time, we are relieved that God does not bring that judgement yet, because we know that others are being gathered into God's family, into the people of God who will gather around his throne in heaven. We are relieved that God is still at work, bringing souls in, but it is hard to wait for justice to be done.

When the sixth seal is opened, and the "great day of their wrath" has finally come, how wonderful it will be to wear the white robe washed in the blood of the Lamb. That robe symbolizes that we are among the conquerors—those who have survived the wrath of God spent on the earth. Just as the tribes of Israel are sealed with the mark of the Lamb, so the white robes seal the victory and salvation of "a great multitude that no one could number, from every nation, from all tribes and peoples and languages" (Rev 7:9).

» Implications

(Choose one or more of the following to think about further or to discuss in your group.)

- Do you pray, like the martyrs, for the day of God's vengeance to come? If not, why not?

- Do you pray for the rest of God's people (the "fellow servants" of 6:11) to be gathered so that the number is complete? If not, why not?

- People often say that God is ignoring all the evil that takes place in the world. How do these chapters help us respond to this complaint?

- The death of Jesus has made his people 'conquerors', as represented by the white robes washed in the blood of the Lamb.

  - What assurances do conquerors have (7:10, 15–17)?

  - What kind of future awaits them? Read Romans 8:31–39 to expand your answer.

(If necessary, this would be a good place to break the study in two.)

The vision of the trumpets

ONE OF THE TRICKS TO UNDER-standing Revelation is to work out what is happening *when*. Are we reading a linear history of events as they will unfold in the world? Or is this book written in a different style to the usual way history or prophecy is recorded? A quick answer is found by comparing Revelation 6:12-13 and 8:12. Look those two passages up now and read them.

You will have noticed that the two passages present pretty much the same event—the destruction of the sun, moon and stars. In fact, the first passage (6:12-13) presents a more complete destruction of the heavens than does the second one. Clearly, these are not events that take place one after the other. Rather, they are *images* that represent events that are taking place. They are images of the same general event—the judgement of the world by Christ. The various visions that we see in Revelation 6-11—and in other parts of the book, too—are not step-by-step records of the end-times. Rather, they are like different camera angles on the one enormous judgement that is taking place. Each vision (or camera angle) gives us more insight into what is taking place. Each vision adds meaning and spells out more of what is happening.

Read Revelation 8:6–11:19.

Again, read quickly, trying to grasp the scenes that are unfolding rather than stopping with the details.

8. What words would you use to summarize what happens when the first four trumpets are blown (8:7-12)?

Optional question

Some of the imagery in this section is common to apocalyptic writing. What other biblical passages come to mind as you read? (E.g. Joel 2:1-11.)

9. In 9:1-11, who is torturing whom? And what are we told about where the torturers come from? (See also 11:7, 17:8 and 20:1-3.)

10. The millions of mounted troops come from beyond the river Euphrates (9:14). This was the boundary of the territory God promised to Israel (Gen 15:18; Josh 1:4). What does this suggest about the kind of judgement we are seeing with the sixth trumpet blast?

11. What is the reaction of the remaining humans, having survived this torrent of judgement (9:20-21)?

12. In 10:1-11:7, an angel tells us what will take place with the seventh trumpet blast. What is it (10:7, 11:15)?

13. John is told to eat the scroll in a similar manner to Ezekiel. Read Ezekiel 2:8-3:3. Who is Ezekiel addressing, and how might this help us understand who John is addressing in his prophecy in Revelation 11?

14. In 10:8-11, John is once again given a prophecy to speak, which he delivers in 11:1-13. During this time of suffering at the hands of the godless nations, what is going to happen:

- in the temple (vv. 1-3)?

- before the Lord (vv. 4-6)?

- in the city street (vv. 7-10)?

- after this (vv. 11-13)?

15. The "two witnesses" are described as olive trees and lampstands. How do the following passages help us understand them?

- Zechariah 4:1-6

- Revelation 1:12-13, 20

- Deuteronomy 19:15

16. In the hymn of thanksgiving that the elders sing (11:17-18), what has God finally achieved?

THE VISION OF THE SEVEN TRUMPETS has added more layers of meaning and understanding to the earlier vision of the seals on the scroll. There are points of overlap between the visions, as we have seen, and both visions keep drawing us back to Old Testament prophecy in order to help us understand that the desire of ages past is being fulfilled—God is condemning the unbelievers and keeping his promises to his people. We have seen a great description of what is to occur—a great and terrible description, for it involves the judgement of the world and the suffering of the church before the glorious appearance of Jesus as king over all.

We must ask God for the endurance and faith to be among those who will overcome.

» Implications

- Is it right or wrong to use 'scare tactics' in evangelism—that is, to warn people of the coming judgement of God?

- Are you willing to suffer persecution for being a Christian, before your resurrection day?

» Give thanks and pray

- Thank God for being a God of justice and mercy.
- Thank God for providing us with a certain refuge from the coming wrath if we trust in his son, Jesus.
- Think of Christian people you know who are suffering for their faith. If you are in a study group, you might like to share your own sufferings. Pray for these people, and for each other, that you would all endure and remember the reality of heaven that is being unveiled.

Endnote
1. This is a long study which may need to be done over two sessions. However, for the sake of the structure of the section, we have left it as one study.

» STUDY 5

POWERS AND AUTHORITIES

[REVELATION 12–14]¹

1. What have you heard about the meaning of the number 666?

IN FRANZ KAFKA'S NOVEL *The Trial*, the main character, 'K', is very confused. He lives in a nightmare world where no-one explains the rules to him. He is dragged off to court to be tried for he doesn't know what, under laws he has no idea about. K's experience has become something of a metaphor for contemporary existence—it's baffling, it can seem random and unfair, and we don't really know what is going to happen next. Someone else (the government, the market, the employer) seems to be in control and they don't necessarily have our good at heart. We feel like we are cogs in a large, unfeeling machine.

Revelation was written to the same kind of world—a decadent world in which governments were corrupt power mongers, innocents suffered, and people feared for their safety. When people say it is hard to understand Revelation because it was written to such a foreign culture, they seem to have forgotten that we have these things in common with our first-century brothers and sisters—we're involved in power struggles. Chapters 12-14 propel us into the heart of these struggles, by revealing the conflict that takes place in heaven as well as on earth.

Signs and times

In the last study, we mentioned the value of modern technology for understanding Revelation—that is, we said that the idea of camera angles is a great help! It is useful here, too, because the events that unfold in chapters 12-14 aren't necessarily happening one after the other. For instance, Revelation 12:1-6 summarizes the events of the rest of the chapter. Notice how the fall of Satan and his angels from heaven is mentioned briefly in verse 4 (with the "stars of heaven" symbolizing the angels), but then expanded for us in verses 7-12. Similarly, the child ascends to God in verse 5, and this is further recounted in verse 14. And his mother flees to the wilderness in verse 6, and this is described to us in more graphic detail in verses 15-16. The later explanations are like action replays of the events, from different camera angles and with further commentary.

Read Revelation 12.

Again, read quickly, noticing the unfolding story.

2. In verses 1-6, what are we told about:

   - the woman?

   - the dragon?

   - the child?

3. In verses 7-12:

   - Who exactly wins the battle over the dragon ("who is called the devil and Satan")?

   - How does Satan fight?

   - How is the battle won?

4. What does Revelation 12 tell us about when the battle in heaven took/takes place?

5. What are the consequences of Satan's expulsion from heaven for:

- the heavens?

- the earth and sea?

6. How successful is the dragon on earth? What does Satan do?

7. Who is the dragon intent on attacking on earth?

LET'S CONSIDER SOME OF THE symbols in this chapter. Roman Catholics identify the woman clothed with the sun as Mary, Jesus' mother. At first this seems an obvious reference, but it is too narrow. Instead, it makes more sense to think of the woman as Israel, the bride of God, who gives birth to the Messiah. The child is clearly a saviour, with the allusion to Psalm 2:9 ("rule all the nations with a rod of iron"). And we are told directly that the dragon represents Satan, so the players in this divine drama are not too difficult to identify. The course of events is only a little more of a challenge.

When was the dragon defeated? Was it before Adam and Eve sinned? Was it at the cross? Is it on the judgement day at the end of the world? The 'when' question is not the Bible's question. The Bible is concerned with telling us that it is certain. The devil is, and will be, defeated. He hasn't got a hope. Why? Because God ordained it to be so. Satan's power is fleeting, and it crumbles in the face of the blood of the Lamb and the faithful testimony of the Lamb's followers (Rev 12:11). Jesus confirms this in Luke 10 when he tells his disciples, who have been announcing the kingdom of God, "I saw Satan fall like lightning from heaven" (Luke 10:18).

Satan is "furious" (12:17), with the fury of a shamed opponent. At the end of chapter 12, he stands by the sea and calls out to it for help in his hopeless battle against God's people. This is the subject of chapter 13.

Read Revelation 13.

Again, note the way the account develops rather than the symbolic details.

8. What kind of authority is given to the beast of the sea, and for how long?

9. Daniel 7 describes four beasts, in a manner similar to Revelation 13 (if you have the time, you might read the chapter). Read Daniel 7:17-18. What is the explanation of Daniel's vision? How might this help us to understand the beast in Revelation 13?

10. How do the people of God fare against the beast?

11. What is the message of verse 10?

12. Compare the first beast (from the sea) with the second beast (from the earth).

- In what ways is the second beast *similar* to the first (vv. 11-12)?

- How does the second beast *differ* from the first (vv. 11-18)?

13. Summarize what the second beast does in the following verses:

- v. 12

- v. 13

- v. 14

- v. 15

- vv. 16-17

14. What do you need in order to conquer the beast and its number (v. 18)? (See also Daniel 11:29-35, 12:10.)

The number of the beast

What a distraction this has been for Christians! This symbol, while striking and thought-provoking, doesn't deserve the conflict and trauma that surrounds it. Like other numbers in Revelation, 666 is a symbolic number.

Three approaches have been taken to its meaning:

1. It is numeric code (*gematria*) for an individual. Since Greek and Hebrew letters have numeric value, this is a fair approach. Revelation 13:18 tells us that "it is the number of a man", suggesting it may represent an individual. But this is of little help to our understanding—it is too easy to make the numbers add up to the name of a vast array of historical figures. This approach has limited value for understanding the message of the book.

2. It refers to a contemporary oppressive world system, either economic or military. This approach makes much ▶

THIS CHAPTER IS ONE OF THE MOST discussed in the Bible—and one of the most abused. It tells us an incredibly graphic story with frightening outcomes; it is no wonder that **'the number of the beast'** has held great appeal for makers of horror films. It is, in fact, just one part of the unfolding story of the journey of Satan and his angels towards their certain judgement.

In this part of the story, two beasts assault the people of God. The dragon and the two beasts[2] are all similar in that they have tried to usurp the authority of God and God's right alone to be worshipped (see 12:10, 13:6, 13:12). Whether they represent a particular power (such as Nero) or government in general, they don't belong there. And, like the dragon, the beasts have this authority on borrowed time: their demise is certain. Revelation 13:7 tells us that the first beast was "*allowed* to make war on the saints and to conquer them". True authorities don't need to ask permission. However, the beasts will wreak suffering and oppression to the point that people will be captured and slain, and the saints will have to endure. This message is constant throughout Revelation: Christians must endure what is to come, and they will then conquer and be rewarded.

Harvest time

If reading Revelation 12-13 is like watching a horror movie, reading chapter 14 is like turning on the lights. It is the moment in which the false rule of the dragon and the beasts is brought to an abrupt and violent halt; it is also the time when the suffering of the faithful—those with the mark of the Lamb—comes to an end. In other words, it is judgement time (14:7).

Read Revelation 14.

Remember to read for the story, not the details.

15. Who is with the Lamb, and where are they gathered?

16. What is the spiritual meaning of being a "virgin" (vv. 4-5)?

of the fact that without the mark no-one can buy or sell (13:17). However, this is best thought of as part of the overall oppression of Christians—it is another way in which they suffer for resisting evil.

3. It is symbolic—a number that represents an idea. As long as we do not ignore the historical issues connected with the book (such as its connections with Daniel 7 in the Old Testament, and the trials and difficulties of the seven Asian churches of chapters 1-3), it seems most fruitful to think of the number communicating a general idea such as oppression, rather than anything more specific.

What does the passage tell us? It tells us that the mark is either a name or number (v. 17). It tells us that it is a mark of belonging to the beast. It tells us that it is a form of slavery to the beast, since without it people will starve and be ostracized.

There is a good deal of 'marking' in Revelation. The servants of God are "sealed" on their foreheads (7:3, 14:1, 22:4); those who oppose God, who practise false religion, also have marks on their foreheads or hands (14:9, 11; 19:20). What matters is whose mark you have: be numbered with the Lamb, not with the Beast.

17. Summarize the actions and the messages of the six angels:

	Actions	Message
vv. 6-7		
v. 8		
vv. 9-10		
vv. 15-16		
v. 17		
vv. 18-20		

18. What kind of harvest is taking place? (See Ps 7:11; Isa 63:3-6; Joel 3:13; Acts 17:30-31.)

Read Isaiah 24:21-23.

19. In what ways is Revelation 14 telling us that Isaiah's prophecy has been fulfilled?

THE CONSEQUENCES OF OPPOSING God, the Lamb and his followers are extremely dire. Anyone who sets himself up against the true and living God is foolish, and his days are numbered. This is as true on a macro scale (in government, in economics) as it is on a micro scale (in the lives of individuals). Worshipping the created order rather than the Creator is the ultimate folly.

What happens to those who do so? They drink the wine of God's fury—they are judged. And this judgement is ordained by the Son of Man, the one who stands among the lampstands (his churches) and vindicates those who keep his commandments and have faith in him (14:12).

» Implications

(Choose one or more of the following to think about further or to discuss in your group.)

- In your own situation, what particular threats to your faith do you face from:
  - government?

- false religion?

- In what ways can Christians stand against the beast and avoid its number? (Consider 13:9-10.)

- Do you fear the oppression that these chapters talk of? If so, how can you strengthen your faith?

» Give thanks and pray

- Thank and praise God for protecting his people and defeating Satan.
- Pray for the endurance and faith of the saints—for you, for your church, and for Christians all over the world.
- Pray for the salvation of people who do not yet trust in Jesus Christ—your family, your friends, and people all over the world. Ask God for boldness to speak about the coming judgement.

Endnotes
1. This is a detailed study. You may like to spread it over two sessions.
2. The second beast is also the "false prophet" of Revelation 19:20 and 20:10.

THE END OF JUDGEMENT

[REVELATION 15–16]

1. Share a situation, either from recent news or from your own life, where justice was not done.

How to do justice God's way

SINCE THE TERRORIST ATTACKS IN America on 11 September 2001, the quest for justice and retribution has been a feature of the daily news headlines. In these chapters, we see the way in which God pursues justice. God is angry—justly angry—and so he punishes those who have sinned, opposing him and bringing about injustice. It is a difficult passage to read, but also a very reassuring one, because it reveals to us the holy character of God.

Punishment can seem awful, but *lack of punishment* is much worse. How terrible is it when a murderer seems to get away with his actions through some legal loophole? Doesn't it heat the blood when it looks like justice will not be done? In these chapters, we see the fulfilment of God's plans to punish the world for its opposition to him and to his people.

Read Revelation 15–16.

Again, read quickly through the details.

2. Compare the song of Moses in 15:3-4 to Exodus 15:1-18. What specific details do the two passages share? What kind of scene does this set for us?

The holy sanctuary

Notice how profoundly holy God is. We may put 'All welcome' signs outside our churches, but the sign across God's sanctuary says "No-one impure can enter here". It is a powerful reminder of just how offensive our sin is to a holy and righteous God. In the final judgement, he will not tolerate any impurity.

3. What has to happen before anyone can enter the **sanctuary** of God?

4. List the reasons for which God is pouring out his wrath in 16:2-7. Who has sinned, and what have they done?

5. What stands out about what happens when the fourth and fifth bowls are poured out?

6. Revelation 16:12-14 contains some unusual imagery. How do the following Old Testament references shed light on their meaning?

- Exodus 8:6-7, 14:21-22

- Isaiah 11:15-16

7. Look up the following references to Armageddon (otherwise known as 'Megiddo'). How do they help us understand why the battle of nations will take place there?

- 2 Kings 9:27

- 2 Kings 23:29-30

- Judges 5:19-23

- Zechariah 12

8. Notice how there is a formula of words used in the following 'ultimate disaster' passages: Revelation 4:5, 8:5, 11:19, 16:18–21.

- What about the formula changes from one to the next?

- What might this suggest for the meaning of the judgement in 16:17–21?

In these chapters, we once again see the 'day of judgement' from a different camera angle to the previous accounts. This time, the writer shows us the judgement through the lens of Old Testament judgements such as the plagues on Egypt, the drama of the Red Sea, and the fall of Babylon. He uses carefully chosen Old Testament themes and subjects, most notably the tent of witness (also known as the 'tabernacle') and the sanctuary (or 'temple'). Before anyone can enter God's sanctuary, God's wrath must be displayed and his judgement on sin completed.

In the bowls, we see a sequence of judgement similar to that of the seals and trumpets. The earth is judged (bowls 1-4), evil forces and institutions are judged (bowls 5-6), and then a final cosmic judgement is proclaimed. Before the last bowl is poured out— before justice is fulfilled—there is mention of "the great day of God the Almighty". It will come "like a thief", echoing Matthew 24:42-44 and 1 Thessalonians 5:2. And on that day will be seen the final division of the world into those who are blessed and those who are cursed. We are warned: stay awake, and keep wearing your clothes of righteousness.

God's judgement is revealed

How do we put together these different visions of God's judgement—the seals, the trumpets and the bowls? The first point we have made is that they are not events that happen one after another, rather they are different descriptions of the same events, seen from different angles. The images themselves help us: the broken seals reveal God's plans for judgement; the trumpets announce its arrival; and the bowls finally pour out God's wrath.

Some wonderful assurances come from these chapters of terror and judgement:

- God's wrath comes to an end—justice gets done.
- Believers in Christ are victorious, because God is victorious.
- God is totally holy, zealous for righteousness, and he will bring it about.
- God will give people what they deserve—his wrath will be shown to be just.

Some awful warnings also emerge:

- Those who oppose God continue to choose to do so, to their own peril. They refuse to repent, and so they suffer judgement.

- After judgement, humanity is permanently divided into two groups: the saints, and those belonging to the beast.

We have now had the plans of God revealed through his word: he will judge the world in justice and truth. The world may appear out of control, running amok without any sense of justice being done. However, we have received this revelation of what is taking place: what is now, and what will be when God's timing is fulfilled. With such extraordinary access to God's purpose, what response could we have other than falling to our knees in repentance and faith?

2 Corinthians 7:10 describes true repentance for us: "godly grief produces a repentance that leads to salvation without regret, whereas worldly grief produces death". Let's not be those who wallow in sin, who will not turn back to God and away from our sin—even when we face the certain judgement of God. Instead, let us grieve over our sin in a way that leads to our salvation and liberates us from guilt and shame through the blood of our Lord Jesus.

›› Implications

(Choose one or more of the following to think about further or to discuss in your group.)

- "The God of the Old Testament is a God of anger, but the God of the New Testament is a God of love." From what we have learned in this study, how could you respond to such a comment?

- In 15:4, the people of God sing about all nations worshipping God. However, in 16:19 the nations come under judgement. How can these two teachings fit together?

- Read Psalm 2. In what sense is this psalm fulfilled in Revelation 15–16?

- "The doors of hell are locked from the inside." Do you agree?

- Do you ever struggle with feeling that God's wrath towards sin is not justified? How does Revelation 15-16 help you to think this through?

- Do you have a godly grief for your sinfulness, or are you trapped in either worldly sorrow or bitter opposition to God? What steps can you take to change?

» Give thanks and pray

- Confess your sin to God and to each other, if you can. Repent; ask God for his forgiveness, and thank him for paying the price for your sin with Jesus' blood.
- Ask God to help you trust him more and more each day—especially in making daily decisions to follow him.
- Ask God to give you a deep concern and love for those who are still lost.

» STUDY 7

THE COMPANY WE KEEP

[REVELATION 17:1–19:10]

1. How much truth do you think there is in the saying "Your character is formed by the company you keep"?

A scarlet woman riding a beast

In the last study, we saw God's judgement on the world coming to an end, and the declaration of the coming great day of God Almighty. Revelation 17-19 provides us with some further details on how the great worldly forces of opposition to God undergo their judgement. That is, they spell out what happened when the sixth and seventh bowls of wrath were poured out in 16:12-21. One of the angels who hold the bowls tells the story (Rev 17:1).

And once again, to those assembled in heaven the judgement of the prostitute and the beast is a source of joy, and they break into jubilant song. The reader senses that the wait for justice is almost over; it's almost time for the wedding banquet of the Lamb.

Once again, these chapters draw on many common Old Testament images and names, most notably Babylon, the ancient oppressor of God's people. We shall seek to sort out the significance of Babylon without getting sidetracked from the main story of God's victory.

Read Revelation 17.

2. Where is the prostitute/woman situated (vv. 1, 3, 15) and what is happening to her (vv. 2, 16-17)?

3. Describe the wrongs that the woman in scarlet has committed.

4. What do the following Old Testament passages about unfaithful 'Babylon-like' cities add to the picture?

   - Isaiah 23:15-18

   - Jeremiah 51:9-14

   - Ezekiel 26-28 (skim it)

5. Why do you think John "marvelled greatly" (vv. 6-8)? How does the angel respond?

6. Describe the relationship between the woman and the beast she rides. What is the beast doing now?

7. How much authority do the forces opposed to the Lamb have (vv. 8, 11, 12, 13)?

THERE ARE LAYERS OF MEANING here that need to be peeled back. The prostitute/woman in scarlet represents Babylon—that much we know from the passage itself. But who, if anyone, does Babylon represent? Since the city of Babylon was judged in the past, we assume its name is being used to refer to something else—but what?

An answer is best put together by gathering the pieces of information that the passage gives us about what Babylon is like, and then thinking about the book of Revelation as a whole. This data can be collected by answering the questions on the next page.

Read Revelation 18.

You can also refer back to chapter 17 in your answers.

8. Is Babylon:	Verses that tell you this:
• wealthy or poor?	•
• friendly or unfriendly to the church (prophets and saints)?	•
• powerful or weak?	•

9. What kind of trade does Babylon do? And where does the city seem to be located?

10. Would you say the description of Babylon seems to be realistic (describing an actual place) or symbolic (representing general ideas and attitudes)? What leads you to this conclusion?

Who or what is Babylon the great?

IT IS SAID THAT THERE IS NO HONOUR among thieves, and the nasty companionship between the prostitute and the beast bears this out. The prostitute has deceived nations and blasphemed against God, aided all the while by her malevolent carrier, the power-hungry beast. Caught up in this pathetic attempt at world domination are ten horns and seven heads, representing earthly kings of one kind or another. They get some of what they want—one hour of rule!—but their ambitions lead to them destroying each other. And all the while, God has been completely in control, agreeing to give some authority while his plans are fulfilled (17:17).

So what do these figures represent? As we have seen, we are given quite a lot of explanation within the passage— in particular, direct interpretation of the images by the angel in 17:7-18. However, beyond that we must admit to taking educated guesses. Identifying ancient Rome with Babylon the prostitute certainly has much merit—it explains many of the images. For example, the seven heads are seven hills, like the seven hills of Rome itself. And some scholars of Revelation believe that the beast refers to the Emperor Nero, a great torturer of Christians who was supposed to have returned from the dead (explaining why he "was and is not and is to come" in 17:8).

But this historical interpretation of the passage is not our foremost concern. Its teaching about the victory of God over all the forces that oppose him has meaning far and beyond any particular victory over Rome. The great cosmic story of salvation which is found in Revelation ensures that it surpasses its historical setting and speaks to us today.

There is a strong warning for Christians in this passage of judgement upon the forces that oppose God. In chapter 18, a voice cries out from heaven to God's people in Babylon. It exhorts them not to share in Babylon's sin, to welcome the judgement God is bringing and to "come out of her". There is great danger in the company we keep. In this time of suffering and evil, before God has brought his final judgement, the wealth and opportunity and magnificence of Babylon will seem very appealing—even to Christian people. Her sins and excesses may not seem quite so evil from the inside. The challenge to God's people is to "come out of her".

And yet, we know that separation from the world itself neither fits with the gospel mission to bring more people into God's kingdom, nor is it even possible when we are hampered by sin ourselves. The world is always with us.

It has been the perennial challenge of the church to work out how to be 'in the world but not of the world', or, in the language of Revelation 18, to come out of Babylon while still bearing testimony to Jesus because the time is short.

A war against the Lamb is to take place, and is in fact taking place. Those who share in the sins of the forces opposed to God also share in their fate—the proper and awful judgement of God. Those who side with the Lamb—those who are "called and chosen and faithful"(17:14)—have a different future, as chapter 19 begins to reveal.

Read Revelation 19:1-10.

11. In what way is the bride made ready for the wedding? (See also Isaiah 61:10, Hosea 2:16-23 and Revelation 6:11 and 7:14.)

12. What did John do wrong in Revelation 19:10?

13. Explain in your own words what it means to say that "the testimony of Jesus is the spirit of prophecy" (19:10).

The end is in sight

THERE IS OFTEN A POINT IN A movie where you can sense that it is about to end. Cues are given—the return of a musical motif, the camera panning back into the distance, characters starting to smile at each other. Revelation 19 has this sense about it. The wedding day has arrived, and preparations are being made. The business of establishing justice and righteousness is just about complete. The final scenes are imminent.

And to heighten this sense of rounding off, verse 10 returns us to an idea that was brought up in the first verses of Revelation. This is the testimony of Jesus: he is letting us know what he has seen, and what is soon to take place. It is his prophecy, and it is a prophecy about him, too. It is his wedding that is just about to take place—and verse 9 reminds us that there is nothing better than receiving an invitation to it.

» Implications

(Choose one or more of the following to think about further or to discuss in your group.)

- When you are tempted to follow the sin of the world—in your workplace, your family life, your sports club or somewhere else—how can you 'come out of Babylon'? Discuss together specific temptations and some strategies for avoiding sin.

- People often devise very elaborate interpretations of parts of Revelation, such as this one about the beast and the prostitute. How can you avoid interpretations which claim to know more than is actually revealed to us?

- How can the pathetic picture of the beast and company fighting for an hour's power help you in your own approach to power and ambition?

- Do you rejoice along with the heavenly assembly in God's victory over worldly powers? Or, like the merchants of the earth, is there part of you that will be sad to see them go? Discuss how you can be wholeheartedly on the side of the Lamb.

» Give thanks and pray

- Thank God for his sovereign control of all things, including those who oppose him. Ask him to help you appreciate the comfort this brings.
- Thank God for his perfect judgement.
- Ask God to help you and your Christian friends to resist the temptations of the world, and to wholeheartedly serve God every day, in every thought, action and decision.

A FEAST AND A FIRE

[REVELATION 19:11–20:15]

1. What do you expect to be doing in heaven? How have you come to this view?

THIS PASSAGE PICKS UP THE drama that unfolded when the sixth bowl was poured out. It tells us more about the fate of the beast and the false prophet (the second beast of Revelation 13). It also tells more about what happens to those who bear the mark of the Lamb and have survived the beast's temptations. And it is great news—they rise to be with Christ in rulership over all.

This scene was introduced to us as a wedding supper, but it is unlike any such feast that a human being has previously attended. In this study, we explore why such a seemingly macabre series of scenes—a cannibalistic feast, everlasting punishment in a lake of fire—is a proper fulfilment of Old Testament expectations. We also look at one of the most over-examined subjects of the book of Revelation— the millennium. Is all the fuss about it justified?

Read Ezekiel 39. In what ways is Revelation 19 fulfilling and explaining these Old Testament words of God?

Read Revelation 19:11-21.

2. Christ is described in a flurry of images and ideas. Summarize what we learn about his character and his deeds.

3. What is the significance of the sword in verses 15 and 21? (See also Hebrews 4:12-13 and Revelation 1:16.)

4. How effective is the war effort of the beast and the kings of the earth (vv. 19-21)?

5. Read Deuteronomy 13:1-5 and Revelation 13:11-14. How does the judgement of the false prophet fulfil the Bible's teaching about the fate of those who deny the truth?

The reign of the saints

WE NOW COME TO ONE OF THE MOST disputed passages in the book of Revelation. Chapter 20 presents many of the most powerful end-time ideas and images—the throne of judgement, the book of life, the lake of fire, and the millennium. It provides some of the most exciting and encouraging teaching on the future of Christian believers.

However, we can lose sight of the comfort and encouragement because of the disputes around its meaning.

Before we try to draw conclusions about it, let's look carefully at the chapter itself, thinking all the while about how much good news there is for Christians—and what terrible news there is for anyone opposed to Christ.

Read Revelation 20.

6. Where is Satan chained up? (See also Revelation 9:1-2.)

7. What happens to the souls of the faithful witnesses of verse 4? What are they doing for **a thousand years**?

8. How effective is the mission of Satan and his forces after he is released?

The millennium

Views on the meaning of the 'thousand years' passage (the millennium) have divided Christians for centuries, in a way which is sometimes less than a good advertisement for the fellowship of faith. Some views of the millennium make it so important that only those who agree are in fact in fellowship. It becomes a sign of true belief.

The differences between views hinge on the order of events, where the events take place, and who will end up with their names in the book of life.

There are three basic views:

- **Pre-millennialism:** Jesus will return and limit Satan's power for a period (1000 years). He will raise Christians to life, and they will set up a kingdom of saints on earth. After the thousand years, Satan will be returned to power, a great battle ▶

will ensue and Satan and his forces will be finally destroyed. The rest of the dead will then rise to final judgement before the new heavens and new earth are established.

- **Post-millennialism**: Christians will reign over the earth with Christ, having risen spiritually with him through their conversion. The kingdom of God will begin on earth, either socially and culturally, or by increasingly effective evangelism (especially to the Jews), until the gospel has been preached to all nations before Jesus returns. The dead then rise to judgement, the end comes and the new heavens and earth are established.
- **A-millennialism**: The thousand years is a symbol for this 'in-between age', when Christ has risen but not returned in judgement. Satan is 'bound' because the gospel is being declared with power; judgement will take place when God deems that the time of salvation has ended. Then the new heavens and earth will be established.

The distinctions between these views are subtle, yet they have led to vastly different views between Christians on politics, social action and ▶

9. Who are "the dead" that are being judged here, and what is their fate?

10. What does it mean to say that "Death and Hades" are thrown into the lake of fire? (See Revelation 1:17-18, 6:8.)

Read Daniel 7:9-14.

11. In what ways is this passage similar to Revelation 20:11-15? In what ways is it different?

Reversal of fates

AFTER READING OF GOD'S JUDGEMENT for 14 chapters, seeing it from different angles, on different time-scales and with complex webs of imagery, we have reached its climax. The fate of all creation has been made clear. What an incredible thing it is to have it revealed to us! How could we ever expect more than this revelation of the end of all things? No wonder John would end the ·book (22:18-19) with his warning to anyone who adds to or subtracts from this book.

The great theme of Revelation 20 is the vindication of God's justice. By the end of the chapter, all those who have resisted the beast have joined Christ in reigning over the world. And anyone opposed to Christ has been judged and received a fate that is described in terrible images of permanent punishment.

Special attention is given to the suffering, faithful people of God. What the saints had undergone in Revelation 13—when the beast was permitted to attack and conquer them—is now reversed. The saints become the conquerors, reigning over the forces that had oppressed them. The beast may have taken their lives, but it could not destroy their souls. And now, the beast himself, along with his cohorts, suffers the everlasting fate called the second death.

With such magnificent, cosmic truths to consider, the specific details of who will reign over what and when fade in their significance.

evangelism. Some views have been embraced by cults to justify all manner of cruel and ridiculous practices. For instance, in the 1830s an Englishman called John Nichols Tom declared himself King of Jerusalem, gathered followers and rode around on a white horse seeking to make the streets flow with blood and initiate the millennium. He was killed in a run-in with the local military.[1]

The fact is that many of the questions people ask about the millennium just aren't answered in the passage itself. This is because they are not part of the symbolic universe that John is using to communicate what he has seen. He is not spelling out for us all the order and detail of the final judgement, but he is telling us the *meaning* of what he has had revealed to him. It can be expressed very simply: God wins. Be on the winning team.

>> Implications

(Choose one or more of the following to think about further or to discuss in your group.)

- Do you have assurance that your name is written in the book of life? If not, consider these passages: John 3:16-18, 3:36; Romans 5:1-5, 8:33-39; Hebrews 10:19-23; 1 John 1:8-9.

- Does your understanding of the millennium make a big difference, a little difference, or no difference in the following areas?

  - evangelism

  - holiness of life

  - contentment

  - assurance

  - attitude to other believers

- In what ways has this study affected your answers (i.e. have you changed your view on anything)?

- Do you have an unhealthy fear of, or interest in, the devil and evil forces?

- How does knowing the fate of the devil and his forces affect our own strength and courage?

- "Revelation is more about the punishment of God's enemies than about evangelizing them." Is this true? Discuss it by looking back at pertinent passages (e.g. Revelation 11).

- "We would understand Revelation better if we knew the Old Testament better." How has this study shown this to be true?

- What questions still remain for you on the issues addressed in this study? What other steps can you take to increase your understanding?

›› Give thanks and pray

- Praise and thank God for his generosity to us in making the fate of all creation known through the Lord Jesus Christ and his servant John.
- Thank God for the assurance and comfort there is in knowing that your name is written in the book of life.
- Pray for those you know who don't have this assurance; ask God to reveal the truth to them.
- Pray that God will give you perseverance and insight in working out any questions that you might still have on the issues addressed in this study.

Endnote

1. Arthur W Wainwright, *Mysterious Apocalypse: Interpreting the Book of Revelation*, Abingdon Press, Nashville, 1993, p. 98.

FACING GOD

[REVELATION 21-22]

1. What features of the new creation do you most look forward to? Are there any features of the old creation that you think you will miss?

MOVIES ABOUT HEAVEN ALMOST always seem to be flops. Have you seen any? Did you think they at all captured what it might be like? Winged costumes, shiny doorknobs, perpetually smiling people, strange soft light— somehow they tend to fall short of generating the kind of desirable world that we could happily call heaven. In contrast, movies about experiences of hell seem to work well, and there are plenty of them—war movies, stories of relationship breakdown, the violence and horror genre. All of the vices mentioned in Revelation 21:8 lend themselves to very realistic and powerful films.

We seem to be good at imagining hell, but inadequate to imagine heaven. Revelation 21-22 provides us with a number of very strong images to help us do it. It is made easier because the Bible presents a clear conception of what really matters about heaven: it is where God is willing to dwell with his people. Some astonishing art has been inspired by these last two chapters of the Bible, but nothing comes close to expressing the relationship that awaits us when God comes so close to us that we see his face.

Optional question

In what different ways is God's "dwelling" with his people described in the following passages?

- Leviticus 26:11-13

- 2 Chronicles 6:18-21

- Ezekiel 37:27-28

- Matthew 1:23, 28:20

- 2 Timothy 1:14

- Revelation 21:3-4

Read Revelation 21–22:5.

2. List all the different images used to describe the people of God in this passage. What does this variety suggest about the way we should interpret this book?

3. List the "former things" that will have passed away before God makes the new heaven and earth.

4. What rewards do the conquerors receive (21:7)?

5. Why do you think the names of the twelve apostles are on the walls of the new Jerusalem?

6. What might verses 24 and 26 mean? (See Isaiah 60:3-5, 11-12, 19-20.)

7. 1 Corinthians 13:12 looks forward to a time when we shall no longer see in a mirror dimly. In what ways does Revelation 22:3-5 speak of this time?

8. What is the significance of God's name being on his servants' foreheads? (See Exodus 28:36-38, Revelation 3:12, 7:3 and 14:1 for clues.)

THE PASSAGE DESCRIBING THE NEW Jerusalem alludes to Isaiah 60-66 and Ezekiel 40-48. It does so in a greatly abbreviated manner, as if to say, "All of those prophecies about the temple are all finally being fulfilled here, with God himself becoming the temple. Now the dwelling place of God is with man!"

The purity of the new heaven and new earth is emphasized negatively by saying that nothing unclean may enter it. The time of God's forbearance of sin is past; only judgement remains at this point. So all who remain opposed to

God—practising magic, worshipping idols, being cowardly in the face of persecution, killing and fornicating—now suffer the same fate as the devil in the lake of fire. The Son of Man spoke against many of these sins in his letter to the churches in Revelation 1-3.

But this negative image is overwhelmed by the wonder of the new world. It is a majestic and grand image of a great city, but it is also a familiar and friendly environment. Jesus offers water to the thirsty, and he calls them his sons (21:7). Heaven is not a cold palace, but a family home—somewhere you can rest with no fear of judgement and no curse on yourself or creation.

The new creations in Christ (2 Cor 5:17) have a new dwelling place, suitable for those who wear the white robes of righteousness. It is so suitable that God himself can be there permanently, face to face with his people.

The glass sea which surrounded the throne in Revelation 4:6 and 15:2 has become a river straight from the throne in Revelation 22, with the tree of life either side of it. "There is a river whose streams make glad the city of God", writes the psalmist (Ps 46:4), glad because God pours out his love and forgiveness. In Ezekiel 47, the river flows from the temple out into the nations, and the leaves of the trees along its banks provide healing. Here, in Revelation 22, the river flows from God himself, flanked by the tree of life with its healing leaves. It is a beautiful image of God's kindness.

Wonder and warnings

Revelation finishes with Jesus' voice reassuring John, and therefore John's hearers and readers, that everything in it is true. The account from the one who "is and who was and who is to come" is all trustworthy, and only a fool would ignore such a revelation.

The book of Revelation is about the past, the present and the future. And Christ is the key to each of these—the Alpha and the Omega, the first and the last. The world was created through him and for him (Col 1:16); he is its saviour; he rose victorious from the grave; and he ascended with power to God's right hand to begin his rule as King of kings. That is the past.

In the present, he continues that rule, dispensing the Holy Spirit to all who believe in him, and thereby marking them as belonging to God and destined for resurrection to eternal life. We have seen that he dwells with the churches, the Son of Man among the lampstands (Rev 1:13), and urges them to conquer, to persevere, and wait to receive their reward.

In the future, his position on the throne of heaven—seen by John through Jesus' revelation—will be seen by all. In the future, every knee will bow before him and every believer will look upon his face without fear. And in the future, he will come to judge the world, to judge the evil forces that oppose him, and to be wed to his bride, the church. The wait is nearly over.

Read Revelation 22:6–21.

9. List the verses in this section that come from Jesus via John, and those that come from John himself.

Jesus	John

10. What is John's mistake in verses 8-9?

11. What two blessings does Jesus pronounce? How can you ensure that you receive these blessings?

12. What two warnings does John issue? How can you ensure you avoid the errors he mentions?

» Implications

(Choose one or more of the following to think about further or to discuss in your group.)

- If nothing unclean can enter the new heaven and new earth, how will you be allowed in?

- "The best things of this world will be preserved in heaven, because the Bible says the glory, honour and wealth of nations will be brought in." Do you agree?

- There are eight mentions of the imminent coming of Jesus in the last 15 verses of Revelation. Do you find it easy to believe that Jesus will soon return? Why or why not?

- How have your images and expectations of heaven changed after doing this study?

- What impact does this teaching on the new heaven and the new earth have on the following aspects of your Christian life?

  - evangelism

  - holiness of life

  - contentment

  - assurance

  - attitude to other believers

- Which of John's warnings in 22:6–21 are most pertinent to you?

- How can you make use of Revelation 21-22 to answer the following comments by unbelievers:

  - "Heaven sounds like one long and boring church service."

  - "In heaven, I will finally get my reward for all the good things I've done that no-one noticed."

  - "I hope I'll go to heaven, but they'll have to change the rules to allow me in."

  - "Will heaven be very different from earth, or just a bit better?"

- List three things that these studies in the book of Revelation have made clearer to you.

- List three things you still need to explore, pray about and meditate upon.

›› Give thanks and pray

- Give thanks and praise to God for his trustworthy character. Thank him for loving mankind so much that he sent his own son to redeem us so that we can enter his presence.
- Thank God for the glorious future we look forward to, when we "also will appear with [Christ] in glory" (Col 3:4).
- Ask God to help you to long for heaven, setting your mind "on things that are above, not on things that are on earth" (Col 3:1-2). Ask him to give you this perspective as you go about daily life, and especially as you relate to people who don't know Christ.

> ### Feedback on this resource
>
> We really appreciate getting feedback about our resources—not just suggestions for how to improve them, but also positive feedback and ways they can be used. We especially love to hear that the resources may have helped someone in their Christian growth.
>
> You can send feedback to us via the 'Feedback' menu in our online store, or write to us at PO Box 225, Kingsford NSW 2032, Australia.

APPENDIX

» TIPS FOR LEADERS

SOME FEEL DAUNTED WHEN THEY approach the book of Revelation. It is written in a style that is unusual for many of today's readers. The symbolic language, the spectacular drama and the cosmic perspective of the book can make the reader feel as if it is all too difficult to understand. Furthermore, Christians are often divided about how to understand Revelation, and this can leave individual readers wondering if they will ever work it out for themselves. Some of the most bizarre religious teachings have found their source in this biblical book, and many readers feel frightened of it as a result.

All of these factors need to be addressed by any leader of a Bible study on this book. First, the leader ought to address any of these thoughts or feelings in his or her own approach; he or she will then be able to serve others in the same way.

The first study helps with understanding the *style* of the book: it looks at what apocalyptic literature is, how Revelation is both similar to and different from other apocalyptic literature, and how to read it without getting totally bogged down in the details.

These studies approach the book by concentrating on *the text of the Bible itself* before drawing any conclusions about how to relate it to church history, theological views and the rest of the Bible. This means that issues such as dispensationalism, the millennium, the number of the beast and the identity of the antichrist are in the background rather than being the focus of discussion.

As to the many views that people may hold regarding this book, it would be worthwhile getting people to raise these early on, acknowledging that we need to bring our understanding in line with what we can know from the Bible, and we need to be patient with each other as we sort out the myths from the reality.

People's thinking on judgement, heaven, hell, and the future of the world has sometimes derived from films or novels which distort or ignore Scripture. Try to bring up this fact early in the group's discussion, and create a willingness within the group to re-examine your beliefs in light of God's word.

How to use these studies

These studies have been written to cover the whole of Revelation in nine sessions. This means some rather fast reading through sections of strange symbolism. We believe this is the best way to understand the meaning of the book—since it was most likely read aloud to the early Christian churches (Rev 1:3)—so that the flow of the story, rather than the details, comes across. Having said that, you may need more than the usual one session for study 4 and/or study 5.

There are lots of Old Testament references in these studies. This is deliberate, because we want to get across the important truth that in order to understand the revelation, we need to know the rest of God's word. The Old Testament prophetic books are particularly important. However, we recognize that there will be a good deal of 'Bible-flipping' taking place in most studies. It may be wise to minimize this, in order to save time and not intimidate people with less Bible knowledge. You may need to ask the more experienced Bible readers in the group to find the passages and do most of the reading.

Finally, the focus of these studies is

Jesus Christ—the one who gives the revelation to John, and the one on whom the revelation is centred. If you find a study drifting into strange, unprofitable territory, think about how it can be brought back to focus on the one who is the beginning and the end, the Alpha and the Omega.

Resources for understanding Revelation

There are an enormous number of commentaries and books on Revelation, many of which have a particular 'spin' on the text. Of those that take an approach similar to these studies, Michael Wilcock's *I Saw Heaven Opened* (IVP, Bible Speaks Today series) and William Hendricksen's *More Than Conquerors: An Interpretation of the Book of Revelation* (Baker) are recommended.

Two gigantic scholarly commentaries on the Greek text have recently been published, one by David Aune and one by GK Beale. At the intermediate level, Robert Mounce's *The Book of Revelation* (Eerdmans, NICNT series) is worth a look. Graeme Goldsworthy's study, *The Gospel in Revelation*, is also very valuable: it is now only available in *The Goldsworthy Trilogy* (Paternoster).

On the subject of apocalyptic literature, see the sidebar in study 1 (pp. 11-12).

Matthias Media stocks MP3 CDs of sermons by Phillip Jensen on each chapter of Revelation. For more details, visit our website: www.matthiasmedia.com.au

matthiasmedia

Matthias Media is an evangelical publishing ministry that seeks to persuade all Christians of the truth of God's purposes in Jesus Christ as revealed in the Bible, and equip them with high-quality resources, so that by the work of the Holy Spirit they will:

- abandon their lives to the honour and service of Christ in daily holiness and decision-making
- pray constantly in Christ's name for the fruitfulness and growth of his gospel
- speak the Bible's life-changing word whenever and however they can—in the home, in the world and in the fellowship of his people.

It was in 1988 that we first started pursuing this mission, and in God's kindness we now have more than 300 different ministry resources being used all over the world. These resources range from Bible studies and books through to training courses and audio sermons.

To find out more about our large range of very useful resources, and to access samples and free downloads, visit our website:

www.matthiasmedia.com.au

How to buy our resources

1. Direct from us over the internet:
 – in the US: www.matthiasmedia.com
 – in Australia and the rest of the world:
    www.matthiasmedia.com.au

Register at our website for our **free** regular email update to receive information about the latest new resources, **exclusive special offers**, and free articles to help you grow in your Christian life and ministry.

2. Direct from us by phone:
 – in the US: 1 866 407 4530
 – in Australia: 1800 814 360 (Sydney: 9663 1478)
 – international: +61-2-9663-1478

3. Through a range of outlets in various parts of the world. Visit **www.matthiasmedia.com.au/international.php** for details about recommended retailers in your part of the world, including www.thegoodbook.co.uk in the United Kingdom.

4. Trade enquiries can be addressed to:
 – in the US and Canada: sales@matthiasmedia.com
 – in Australia and the rest of the world: sales@matthiasmedia.com.au

Other Interactive and Topical Bible Studies from Matthias Medi

Our Interactive Bible Studies (IBS) and Topical Bible Studies (TBS) are a valuable resource to help you kee feeding from God's word. The IBS series works through passages and books of the Bible; the TBS series pul together the Bible's teaching on topics such as money or prayer. As at February 2010, the series contair the following titles:

Beyond Eden
GENESIS 1-11
Authors: Phillip Jensen and
Tony Payne, 9 studies

Out of Darkness
EXODUS 1-18
Author: Andrew Reid, 8 studies

The Shadow of Glory
EXODUS 19-40
Author: Andrew Reid, 7 studies

The One and Only
DEUTERONOMY
Author: Bryson Smith, 8 studies

The Good, the Bad and the Ugly
JUDGES
Author: Mark Baddeley, 10 studies

Famine and Fortune
RUTH
Authors: Barry Webb and
David Höhne, 4 studies

Renovator's Dream
NEHEMIAH
Authors: Phil Campbell and
Greg Clarke, 7 studies

The Eye of the Storm
JOB
Author: Bryson Smith, 6 studies

The Search for Meaning
ECCLESIASTES
Author: Tim McMahon, 9 studies

Two Cities
ISAIAH
Authors: Andrew Reid and
Karen Morris, 9 studies

Kingdom of Dreams
DANIEL
Authors: Andrew Reid and
Karen Morris, 9 studies

Burning Desire
OBADIAH AND MALACHI
Authors: Phillip Jensen and
Richard Pulley, 6 studies

Warning Signs
JONAH
Author: Andrew Reid, 6 studies

On That Day
ZECHARIAH
Author: Tim McMahon, 8 studies

Full of Promise
THE BIG PICTURE OF THE O.T.
Authors: Phil Campbell
and Bryson Smith, 8 studies

The Good Living Guide
MATTHEW 5:1-12
Authors: Phillip Jensen and
Tony Payne, 9 studies

News of the Hour
MARK
Authors: Peter Bolt and
Tony Payne, 10 studies

Proclaiming the Risen Lord
LUKE 24-ACTS 2
Author: Peter Bolt, 6 studies

Mission Unstoppable
ACTS
Author: Bryson Smith, 10 studies

The Free Gift of Life
ROMANS 1-5
Author: Gordon Cheng, 8 studies

The Free Gift of Sonship
ROMANS 6-11
Author: Gordon Cheng, 8 studies

The Freedom of Christian Living
ROMANS 12-16
Author: Gordon Cheng, 7 studies

Free for All
GALATIANS
Authors: Phillip Jensen
and Kel Richards, 8 studies

Walk this Way
EPHESIANS
Author: Bryson Smith, 8 studies

Partners for Life
PHILIPPIANS
Author: Tim Thorburn, 8 studies

The Complete Christian
COLOSSIANS
Authors: Phillip Jensen and
Tony Payne, 8 studies

To the Householder
1 TIMOTHY
Authors: Phillip Jensen and
Greg Clarke, 9 studies

Run the Race
2 TIMOTHY
Author: Bryson Smith, 6 studies

The Path to Godliness
TITUS
Authors: Phillip Jensen and
Tony Payne, 7 studies

From Shadow to Reality
HEBREWS
Author: Joshua Ng, 10 studies

The Implanted Word
JAMES
Authors: Phillip Jensen and
Kirsten Birkett, 8 studies

Homeward Bound
1 PETER
Authors: Phillip Jensen and
Tony Payne, 10 studies

All You Need to Know
2 PETER
Author: Bryson Smith, 6 studies

The Vision Statement
REVELATION
Author: Greg Clarke, 9 studies

Bold I Approach
PRAYER
Author: Tony Payne, 6 studies

Cash Values
MONEY
Author: Tony Payne, 5 studies

Sing for Joy
SINGING IN CHURCH
Author: Nathan Lovell, 6 studies

The Blueprint
DOCTRINE
Authors: Phillip Jensen and
Tony Payne, 9 studies

Woman of God
THE BIBLE ON WOMEN
Author: Terry Blowes, 8 studies